BREATHING AGAIN

A HURRICANE HARVEY MEMOIR

RACHAEL VALKA

Unless credited, all images are the work of Rachael & Michael Valka

Cover design by Mike McDonell

Book design created by Rachael Valka with Vellum

ISBN 978-0-692-16253-8 (Print Edition)

ISBN 978-0-692-18991-7 (Ebook Edition)

Printed by Ingram Spark, in the United States of America

First Printing, 2018

For updates or to contact Rachael:
Facebook: Red Light Writings
Email: RedLightWritings@gmail.com

CONTENTS

Spring, TX (August 29, 2017)

"You can do the impossible, because you have been through the unimaginable."[1]

— CHRISTINA RASMUSSEN

INTRODUCTION

From August 25-29, 2017, Hurricane Harvey stalled over southeast Texas unleashing over fifty inches of rain in some parts of the greater Houston area. Tens of thousands of residents were displaced as flood waters rose in what ultimately was one of the wettest and costliest hurricanes to hit the United States. Through the upheaval in its wake, the enduring testimony of Hurricane Harvey remains the strength and resiliency of the human person and the hope found in a community of support. This memoir began as a simple poem to process one of the days of Harvey and quickly grew to capture the stories and emotions of my closest family and friends. For as a woman of faith, their stories become part of my own heart and story. Interwoven in these stories during the days and weeks after Hurricane Harvey are flashbacks to my own life and my simultaneous coping with the acceptance of being severely asthmatic. All of this came to an emotional peak in my life during the days and weeks of this hurricane.

Suffering, as told in this story, bears the many names of natural disasters, chronic illness, loss, brokenness, and so much more. Though suffering is an inescapable part of our common human experience, it finds redemption and hope in the bonds of charity that unite us all as children of God. It is my sincere hope that this memoir of my own heart resonates with these universal human experiences of suffering, hope, and resiliency we all share.

The stories presented here are all my understanding and perception of real life events. Nothing has been added, changed, or exaggerated beyond my what my memory and imagination recall. The characters are all real, as are their stories. Minor characters retain their real names; however, most of the characters are called by a title or a nickname. Capitalization of character names, including titles like Mom and Dad and nicknames like the Saint, was purposefully chosen to help these key characters stand out. They are among my closest family and friends whose stories are interwoven in mine and who have weathered the storms of my life by my side. As this memoir works through its final editing stages, over seven months after Hurricane Harvey hit, many of these dearest people in my life are still in some stage of rebuilding or recovering, physically or emotionally, from this storm. It is my prayer that they, and you the reader, find in these pages a glimmer of hope and healing out of the suffering of life's storms.

WORDS OF THANKS

"I give thanks to my God at every remembrance of you, praying always with joy in my every prayer for all of you."

— PHILIPPIANS 1:3-4

To my husband, the Saint, who knew before I did that this project would bring healing and fill my soul, for your unfailing love, support, and encouragement in all our endeavors of this beautiful life together.

To Older-son, Middle-son, and Younger-son, who infuse our lives with unending light and energy, for bringing a joy and love to our lives we never knew could exist.

To Mom and Dad, who knew me before I knew me, loved me before I loved me, and formed me to be the person I am today, for your steadfast presence, love, and encouragement throughout my life.

To my friends of this story: Frog, Sunshine, and Joy-Bearer, and to all those who have blessed my life in countless ways, for the warmth of friendship that challenges, encourages, weathers my storms, and brightens my soul.

To those whose labors of love helped make this project possible. To Mom and Leslie for being my cheerleaders and editors. To Mike for his encouragement and beautiful cover design. To Morgan and Paper Raven Books for guiding me each step of the way without asking anything in return.

To Heidi who pushed me to finish this book and even more triumphs than I could imagine.

A Day of Yard Clean Up (September 16, 2017)

1

NIGHTMARES

MOM SAYS IT IS THE STUFF NIGHTMARES ARE MADE OF.

I felt it coming. Deep in my chest. An ache. A growing tightness, like a human barometer. I felt it in each asthmatic breath I took barreling uncontrollably towards us.

Have you seen the weather, my husband, the Saint asked?

No, it's the first week of school; I have been busy.

Will the weather explain why my asthma is off?

Your asthma is off? Crap.

There's a storm brewing in the Gulf, he said.

Crap, I sighed.

By the time we felt the first rain bands come through, my asthma was suffocatingly heavy. Exhaustion punished my body before it even started. Tornado alerts sounded all night through the city.

Sirens raged through the streets. The winds and rain beat against the windows. Not like in Corpus, I kept telling myself. Not like in Corpus. We reached a point that night where prayer was all we could muster, all we could do, all we could hope with. Prayer and waiting.

The first light of morning brought unbelievable images. My brother was flooded out of his house. Water three feet deep. Two out of three cars filled with water. A neighbor broke in to rescue their dog while they were gone. They had never flooded with any other storm. They had no words. We had no words. Mom finally said, it's a tale of two hurricanes. I'll take wind over water any day. In Hurricane Ike we moved everything from upstairs down because of the threat of wind and trees taking off the roof. In Harvey we moved everything from downstairs up because of the threat of rising water.

It is the stuff nightmares are made of.

Some people went to church Sunday morning and couldn't get back home into Mom and Dad's neighborhood. Trapped. Out of their house with nowhere to go and nothing but the clothes on their backs. I begged Mom and Dad to leave and come to my house. I pleaded. Late that afternoon the Saint and I finally kayaked in. We filled one kayak with Mom and Dad's belongings and one with their white Labrador retriever. We waded through the chest deep flood waters, pushing the kayaks. It was a somber walk not knowing to what we would return to the next day. At times the only sound was the dog crying. She shook and whimpered. She tried to jump out of the kayak. She could swim, but we waded for almost a half of a mile out. Too far for an old house lab to swim. I soothed her as I steered the kayak in the cold, high water. I petted her head. It's okay, girl. It's okay. A mantra more for myself than the frightened dog.

BABY BOY'S STORY

We were home, clean and dry about an hour. Then Mom got the call. A friend was trapped in her house with her sister and two-year-old nephew as the water was rising into their first floor.

Dad and I looked at each other. We are going. Get the address and tell them we are on our way.

We backed the cars up to the water line and unloaded the boats. Two adult kayaks and one child kayak for the baby or for things. We would just have to see. Dad and I paddled out following Google maps to an unknown home to meet strangers and bring them to safety. It was about a mile of completely flooded waters and twisting and turning roads. Families stood in their garages, water lapping at their doorsteps.

The boats, they called, have you seen the boats?

The boats, are the boats coming?

House after house the same plea.

No, we have not seen the boats.

Up ahead a car slowly drifted through the street lifted by the current. Only the rooftop peeked above the water line. The adrenaline in us failed to see the current we were so easily riding as we pushed past the car.

The rain picked up as we reached Baby Boy's house. We brought a life jacket for him. We hadn't thought about us. His aunt brought him to the door, we buckled the life jacket around him, and I placed him in my lap in the kayak. He shivered in the cold and shook with fear. I held him close to me, wrapping my arms securely around him. As they loaded the other boats, I sang to him the only song in my head. A soothing song we sang in the evenings in the dorms in college. Its rhythm like a lullaby taking us to a place of the comfort and rest in the arms of our Father.

I closed my eyes and smelled his curly baby hair right there in the chaos of that kayak, and I was transported to my own baby boys. To the peaceful moments holding them and smelling their soft baby hair. I was transported to the comfort of college friends back in those dorms, and I reminded myself to fear nothing at all for the arms of my Father hold me safe.

I held him tight and sang it twice as the others checked electrical boxes and loaded the other boats. I made it two houses down before the current pulled so hard that my boat stood still in a battle between the water and my tired muscles.

Get near the houses, Dad called, the current is weaker there.

On the houses and fences crawled insects of every size, color, and shape. All seeking survival. I brought myself to grab the wall and steady us for a moment. I had to get out and try to pull the boat through the current instead. It's okay buddy. It's okay. A mantra more for myself than the frightened child.

The weather started to beat down on us again. Rain and wind. Crosscurrents rose as the creek did. We tied a long cord around Dad as he tried to navigate a swift flowing street. Our last hope was to tie a rope from a tree to a stop sign, so we wouldn't get swept with the current.

We had to turn back. We had to leave them behind shaken, cold, wet, scared, unsure of what would come next. With only the promise that we would give the fire department their address as soon as we saw them. With only the hope that the boats would eventually come.

The defeated kayak trip back was treacherous and exhausting, even for Dad and me who are mentally and physically strong. Darkness was falling upon us fast.

Daughter, we will start upstream and aim for that tree while we paddle as hard as we can across this street. Hopefully, we will make it across before we hit that point over there.

Get along the fence line. It breaks the current up.

Dad grab this tree and rest a minute.

We both need a little breather.

The rain pelted our arms, legs, eyes. We joked about getting a junior white-water hurricane badge. We joked about father-daughter bonding. Anything to take our minds off the tiring trek back, off our failed attempt to help, off our worries about the countless people stuck out there waiting for the countless boats we had not seen.

As we turned the last corner, we saw Mom through the darkness wading in chest deep water in a panic for us. Have you seen two kayaks back there, Mom was asking each person coming out? Two yellow kayaks with a man and a woman? She was on the phone praying with a friend. I know they are strong and good swimmers, but I heard that the water was too bad to even help people out. Where are they, she pleaded?

I called out to her. Mom! What are you doing? What do you think you were going to do?

Find you, she shouted! I was coming to find you!

Mom! Turn around, don't drown!

The county campaign to not drive in high water was the only joke I had left in my tired, achy, defeated body.

I drove home in silence. Trying to process.

It is the stuff nightmares are made of. We reached a point that night where prayer was all we could muster, all we could do, all we could hope with. Prayer and waiting.

Close to midnight we got a call. She sent her sister and Baby Boy upstairs while she stood on her porch with a lantern. Water rising to her calves, thighs, waist. Waiting for the boats.

The boats, are the boats coming?

No, we have not seen the boats.

The boats finally came. Rescued by the fire department, they were now sitting in a warehouse waiting for a bus to a shelter. Waiting. Without hesitation: we are coming. The strangers we left behind over high, fast-moving waters now felt like family. We are coming. The Saint and I set up more beds while Mom and Dad picked them up. Mom brought Baby Boy in shivering with cold, shaking with fear. We drew him a warm bath and got him in pajamas. I held him on the couch now with a soft, warm blanket. He had a cookie and milk, and I sang a *Moana* song with Netflix playing while his mom and aunt got dry, clean, and warm. As I sang, I thought about each of us at the edge of our waters, and I wondered just how far all this will go. How far will each of us go?

The next morning, we called our home the hotel Valka, a bed and breakfast, with pancakes, eggs, and coffee to go around. They went to stay with a friend, and we went to check on Mom and

Dad's house. All of us tired, weary, and unsure of what the future would hold as the rain kept coming day after day.

A NEIGHBORHOOD STORY

The sound of helicopters rumbling through the sky filled the air day in and day out. It was still raining when we went back to Mom and Dad's house. The water was still rising as we kayaked in to their little island. The house was still above the water line. But the water was rising three inches an hour shrinking the island and threatening their house. We moved more stuff upstairs and walked around with hands at our waist imagining water levels.

What would be destroyed if it was this high?

How about this high? It can't possibly get this high, can it?

It can. Who knows. Who knows anything anymore.

Please, it can't go any higher than this.

Can we just save this level and down?

We walked around, hands waist high, imagining the threatening water levels.

What supplies will help us if this keeps going?

What food, what cleaners, what clothing?

More time to think today than yesterday. Still can't stay long.

The water was rising three inches an hour, maybe more.

We connected the kid kayaks to the adult ones and towed them out with coolers and bags filled with supplies.

How long do you think you will be out of the house?

How much do you think we will need?

Who knows. Who knows anything anymore.

Watch out for the mailbox over there.

Somewhere over there is a brick mailbox. You can't see it until you are right up on top of it. The water line is just over it. Watch out. If you scrape it, it will knock you off balance. Each time in and out we watched and signaled each other with the hazards we knew. What hazards lay beneath unaware to us? What horror still lay hidden in this mess?

The rain and wind picked up again on our second trip. This is it Dad. We need to go. Last trip. Whatever you can fit in this trip is it. The weather is getting bad again. We are tired. Last trip.

With rain pelting our bone-tired, soul-weary group, we left the little island not knowing what tomorrow would bring.

It is the stuff nightmares are made of. We reached a point that night where prayer was all we could muster, all we could do, all we could hope with. Prayer and waiting.

The water was glass the next day. The little island held. The water peaked at the roof eaves of many houses and slowly started to recede. It smelled like the fishing trips I remember from childhood. Not like fish yet, but that freshwater lake smell. The smell of the greatness, the primitiveness, the power of mother-nature now filled my childhood streets. Memories converged in a confusing swirl of emotions. Lake trips to Grandma and Grandpa's house now mixed with bike rides down these river-like streets. What is this place I am rowing through? This unfamiliar space overwhelms me.

~

THE ANGER STORY

Hurricanes do not discriminate. They unleash their fury, driving their wind, dumping their rain, swirling their power over us all. Hurricanes do not discriminate. Or do they?

As the story played out, the vulnerable, weaker, less fortunate among us are the ones hit hardest. Those who are higher educated with the means have land on higher ground. And insurance. The flood waters took the lowest land first and the least among us. I saw a news article: morgues overflowing after the wake of Harvey. Clever headline. Heart-breaking headline. But the news isn't reporting hundreds of victims. Who are these nameless faces filling the morgues?

My co-teacher, Joy-Bearer, texted. Her friend's mom was evacuated from the nursing home. Elderly. Frail. Suffering from dementia. She passed away right after the transfer. Slipped away from the family as the waters rose around us.

And the homes gone with story after story of people who lost everything, who had nothing. Someone said eighty percent didn't have insurance. I don't know about that. They say it was a thousand-year flood. Who would buy insurance with those odds? But eighty percent? The sentiment is not off. So many. Too many. Without home. Without insurance. Barely anything to begin with. Now nothing. Those with higher education and means have land on higher ground. And insurance. It is a poverty cycle issue. Another example of the least among us stuck in suffering. Where do they go from here? How do they ever get back on their feet when they were barely standing, barely breathing to begin with?

The Saint said that's not fair. Hurricanes don't discriminate. Look at the west side. He reminded me that we used to work over there. We know those people. We served them when we worked at the Church. A taxed reservoir was relieved right into their neighborhood. Water from the reservoir spewing out, filling homes. Evacuations because the water just stopped flowing. Water still standing weeks after Harvey came and went. I imagined family after family still having to wade or boat into their homes while the rest of the city was drying out, moving on. I thought about them, forgotten. Stuck. In a stagnating cesspool of destruction and disease.

Perhaps it's not fair. But then again. None of it is.

And city planning. Homes built where they should not be built. Stop building on creeks that flood. Stop building levees to protect a few at the expense of everyone upstream. The levees made a dam that blocked the water, forcing it into other neighborhoods. Rising higher and higher like my anger at the cycle of suffering.

Rising above the waters just to be pushed back down.

Over and over again.

We heard Spring was hit hard, they called. How are you?

We are fine, but Spring was hit hard. How are you?

Oh, we are great, they say.

Great? How can anyone be great at a time like this?

Higher land. Insurance.

Death. Destruction. Ruin. Poverty. Stagnating water.

Cycling over and over.

It is the stuff nightmares are made of.

SURVIVOR'S GUILT

I can't just keep sitting here doing nothing, one friend said. I feel so helpless. So guilty.

There are just lots of people with lots of trauma, another friend texted. Much more than I have. None.

I kind of have some survivor's guilt, so many said.

So, I looked it up on Wikipedia. Survivor's guilt: "a mental condition that occurs when a person believes they have done something wrong by surviving a traumatic event when others did not." It is driving some people crazy in this chaos. Driven to give, driven to help, driven to do anything so as not to be driven crazy. It haunts them.

Joy-Bearer started crying on the phone as she described it to me. Pot Roast. We're having pot roast for dinner. Our house is dry and warm. We just watch the news. We are fine, but we can't get to anyone. But it feels not right, you know. Eating pot roast while everything around us is in chaos. We just watch and wait and pray. She recalled a story from the previous day.

We waited in line for an hour and a half for our groceries. We had nothing else to do. Then a man came up and offered ten dollars for our milk. Ten dollars!

I just need some milk for my baby at home. All I have is a ten. I'll give you ten dollars for your milk, he said.

No, she said.

I'm sorry, he retreated wounded.

No, she said, I mean, no you can't pay me. Take both gallons.

Take whatever you need. You can't pay me, take my groceries, I'll get more.

This generosity from the same woman who offered to pay me a hundred dollars because we were buying a new mattress to house a family. You know, her voice drifted reflectively, we can't leave the house alone. We have stuff. There is looting. I worry we are targets now. We who survived.

The restlessness. The anxiety. The helplessness. Survivor's guilt.

It is the stuff nightmares are made of.

THE CANCER STORY

He posted, please pray for my daughter today. She is supposed to have her next round of chemo, but the hospitals are flooded. We will have to postpone treatment. We will have to wait.

Oh, the waiting is the worst. Your mind plays games as it starts to imagine the tumors growing instead of shrinking because you are waiting. My heart ached for him, his wife, his beautiful daughter. Stuck. Waiting.

In his plea for prayer, I remembered our waiting like it was yesterday. My memory drifted back to that morning I found the Saint walking along the side of a busy road.

Surgery is cancelled, he said. No surgery today.

I know, I said, get in the car.

I had dropped him off for pre-op earlier that morning.

I got the kids settled at school and headed back to be with him.

He called, no surgery today. Come pick me up.

I rushed back to the surgery center, and he was gone. He just walked out of pre-op and kept walking for miles towards home. He couldn't sit there; he couldn't be with himself or his thoughts any longer.

I picked him up walking along the side of the road.

Surgery is cancelled, he said. No surgery today.

I know, I said, get in.

It's not a cyst, he said. They can't operate.

What is it, I asked tentatively?

Don't know. Have to go to MD Anderson to find out.

We rode in silence the rest of the way home. Processing.

We waited for answers. For weeks. Everything else seemed trivial. I saw myself as a single mom with three kids. Younger-son wasn't even a year old yet. The waiting is the worst. The Saint does not have sarcoma like they initially thought. He had a year of chemotherapy and surgery and now checks on his disease every six months.

I think about that mom when I was a kid. Was it breast cancer? Was it brain cancer? The memories all fade together for a young child. Mom made her meals. Her son went to my school. I remember his name: Chris. I remember her face: swollen round as a moon, no hair, scarf draped over her head. In a matter of months this kid at my school had no mother. What would happen if I had no mother?

I think about that mom last spring. She was another college friend's wife. Mother of four. My age. Stage four cancer. Cancer came. Cancer went. Cancer came. Cancer took. Her funeral was standing room only. A testament to a life infused with faith, hope, and love. A testament to a life of courage and grace. A testament to a life mourned and lost too young with too much work left to do. Like some Latin phrase from Julius Caesar deep in the recesses of our school year memories, cancer proclaims its tyrannical warning to us all. *Veni. Vidi. Vici.* Cancer bears a striking resemblance to hurricanes.

I can't stop thinking about the cancer patients today. Their hospital with water through the first floor. Their treatments, postponed. Their endless days of unknown, perpetuated. Their only normalcy of scheduled visits and therapies, on hold. The what-ifs. The guilt. The fear. The anguish. The survivor's guilt fills me for all of them as I try to sleep. I can't stop thinking about my college friend. I can't stop thinking about his daughter. Osteosarcoma. Stage four. Stuck. No treatments. Postponed. I closed my eyes and prayed for them. Prayer and waiting.

Motherless children. Childless mothers.

Cancer.

It is the stuff nightmares are made of.

STEVE'S STORY

Some stories are too deep, too personal to loved ones that I fear I do not have the words to tell them. I fear my words will never capture the heartbreak Harvey wrought.

Frog texted: my dad fell and has been on the floor since last night. Please pray someone can get to him.

Where do you begin to find words beyond prayer?

He made it to a hospital only to be evacuated to another one.

I imagined him lying there on the floor, a man I've never met, scared, helpless, cold. I imagined his family, scared, helpless, numb. I imagined him in a hospital bed and in a helicopter evacuating across the city, alone. I imagined his family stranded, fighting high water and closed roads to get to him, alone. I closed my eyes that night and prayed for him and for them with every tight achy breath I had. It's okay, friend. It's okay. A mantra more for myself than my frightened friend.

It is the stuff nightmares are made of.

Text after text came in over the days of Harvey as he slowly slipped away from them.

Frog texted: It's the end. I prayed with him and said goodbye.

Jesus, I trust in you. The only words left in my aching heart.

She is my best friend, and this hell called Harvey means the other side of the city may as well be the other side of the world. It sure feels like it. No words over text can comfort like the warmth of a hug. No words over text can sustain like the presence of a soft hand. No words will suffice anymore. I reached a point that night where prayer was all I could muster, all I could do, all I could hope with. Prayer and waiting.

I prayed her a distant lullaby from my college dorms about the comfort and rest of our Father. I prayed her Baby Boy's lullaby to fear nothing at all for the arms of our Father hold them all safe.

Frog texted: he's gone.

Prayer. The only words anyone has left.

And they have fallen into silence.

Silence and waiting.

She texted: I can't even pray.

Yes friend, I've been there a couple times already this week.

Today I will be your voice of prayer.

Prayer. Found now only in the deepest spaces of the heart.

The words of tradition are all that remain.

Eternal rest grant unto him, O Lord, and let perpetual light shine upon Him.

May his soul and the souls of all the faithful departed, through the mercy of God, rest in peace. Amen.

"And Jesus wept."[2]

"He got into a boat and his disciples followed Him. Suddenly a violent storm came upon the sea, so that the boat was being swamped with waves; but He was asleep. They came and woke him, saying, 'Lord, save us! We are drowning!' He said to them, 'why are you terrified, O you of little faith?' Then he got up and rebuked the winds and the sea, and there was a great calm."[3]

It is the stuff nightmares are made of.

Won't someone go wake up our Lord?

On the way to "Baby Boy's" house (August 27, 2017)

A car floating in the current (August 27, 2017)

A makeshift "bed & breakfast" room for three (August 27, 2017)

A makeshift "bed & breakfast" room for Mom and Dad (August 27, 2017)

A rainy trip to get supplies (August 28, 2017)

~

A flooded truck and other road hazards (August 28, 2017)

A flooded house with rain still coming (August 28, 2017)

~

Dad making a trip to get supplies (August 29, 2017)

The neighborhood with no streets (August 29, 2017)

A flooded house with water receding (August 29, 2017)

The Marine Corps veteran's house (August 29, 2017)

The view from around the neighborhood (August 29, 2017)

"Yard of the Month" (August 29, 2017)

Watching out for street signs (August 29, 2017)

A flooded car with flags on the submerged fence (August 29, 2017)

Passing the same truck (August 29, 2017)

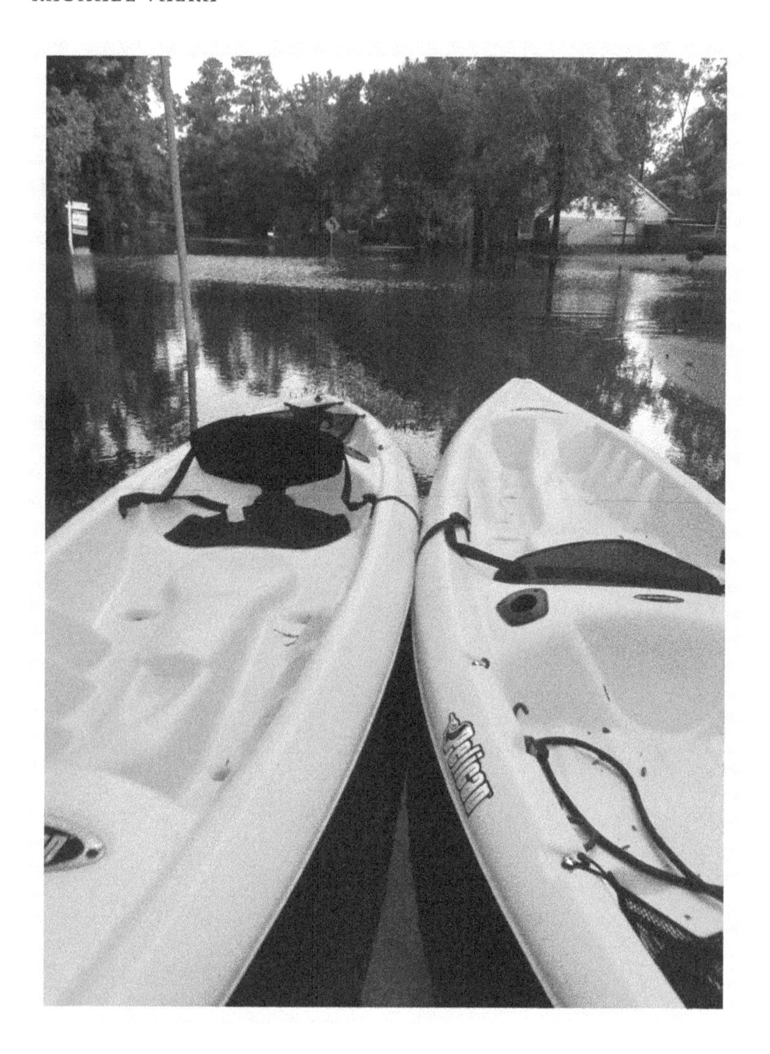
Pelican

2

ISLANDS

Mom says we are all islands right now.

When we feel hopeless and overwhelmed by the scope and gravity, we need to remember that all we can do right now is focus on our own island and take good care of each other on this island.

Mom says we are all islands right now.

And we find that out of the worst of nightmares hope and grace shine brightest.

All told, I kayaked about seven to eight miles in forty-eight hours. On our last kayak trip to Mom and Dad's house, we brought a gas can in to start a generator, checked the property, and grabbed a few more supplies.

We met some guys from Waco. They bought a bass boat and traveled to Houston. They were there to bring anyone out, bring anything in to those trapped, and patrol for safety. They were there to do whatever they could.

As we pushed off the now growing island, a ray of sun peeked through the clouds. Water kept slowly receding as the sun burst through the clouds pushing away the grey and revealing jewel blue skies with white puffy clouds turning soft pink as the sun began to set. Old Glory waved from the second story of a submerged house. The first signs of hope in days for a battered city. Hope was finally rising faster than the waters. That night we sat in the middle of my dry street watching the sun set and Harvey's final rain bands make their slow circular push eastward.

THE UNSUNG HEROES

The Waco bass boaters weren't the only ones to spring into action. They came from Austin with two jet skis and pulled person after person out from the Addicks and Katy areas. When one jet ski lost battery power, he kept going in alone while his brother offered first aid to victims brought out. They are close family friends. The Saint's boss and his brother.

He left our island wedged between two swelling creeks to buy a jet ski and couldn't get back. They closed each creek crossing as he tried to get home. Route after route blocked. They closed the last freeway entrance just as he came up to it. He was stuck in a shelter for the night. Trapped off his island. Trapped next to a levee threatening to succumb to Harvey at any minute. The next morning the police escorted him to the Lake Houston area where he spent hours on his new jet ski pulling person after person to dry land before he finally made it home to our island that night, exhausted. He is my uncle.

Her house was a constant buzz with four children. But she heard about their family. Kazakhstani immigrants who lost everything in the flood. I have the room; they can stay here. In the moments of deciding, they found other housing. Opening her doors to strangers as so many across the city did, coordinating donations and monetary collections for our brother who got flooded, for friends, for complete strangers. She is my sister.

"Then the king will say to those on his right, 'Come, you who are blessed by my Father. Inherit the kingdom prepared for you from the foundation of the world. For, I was hungry and you gave me food, I was thirsty and you gave me drink, a stranger and you welcomed me, naked and you clothed me, in prison and you visited me. Then the righteous will answer him and say, 'Lord when did we see you hungry and feed you, or thirsty and give you drink? When did we see you stranger and welcome you, or naked and clothe you? When did we see you ill or in prison, and visit you?' And the king will say to them in reply, 'Amen I say to you, whatever you did for these least brothers of mine, you did for me.'"[4]

These unsung heroes represent the countless others who sprang into action driven by the desire to help their fellow man. Driven by the sense that we are all one human family connected and here to help each other. They didn't wait, didn't think twice, didn't hesitate. As the storm raged and the waters rose, they did not wait. In the blink of an eye, they served the frightened among us. Without hesitation.

Stranger helping stranger. Cor Unum. One Heart.

THE SPRING HIGH SCHOOL STORY

The district officials didn't wait, didn't think twice, didn't hesitate. They opened the school to anyone, in the district or not. The community didn't wait, didn't think twice, didn't hesitate. Within a matter of hours, they were offering warm food, shelter, clothing, beds to anyone who could get there. Teachers operated a child care area, district nutritionists came to run the food service center, district police officers kept peace and order, technologists opened the computer lab for FEMA help, the whole community filled volunteer shifts within a matter of minutes.

He walked into the shelter from Alcoholics Anonymous.

Can I hold a meeting here tonight for anyone who needs it?

Really?? These people need food, shelter, warmth.

Wait. These people need care in the deepest places of their hearts.

"When Jesus raised his eyes and saw that the large crowd was coming to Him, He said to Philip 'Where can we buy enough food for them to eat?' He said this to test them, because He Himself knew what He was going to do. Philip answered Him, 'Two hundred days wages worth of food would not be enough for each of them to have a little bit.' Andrew said to Him 'There is a boy here who has five barley loaves and two fish; but what good are they for so many?' Jesus took the loaves, gave thanks, and distributed them to those who were reclining, and also as much fish as they wanted. When they had had their fill...they collected [the leftovers] and filled twelve wicker baskets with fragments from the five barley loaves that had been more than they could eat."[5]

The community kept coming. Restaurants with catered meals, bags piled upon bags of linens, clothing, toys, shoes, air mattresses. The high school shelter was now ground zero in Spring to send donations to the wider community. Trucks and SUVs loaded to capacity with trip after trip to neighboring churches ready to act as local distribution sites. A caravan of army vehicles with water bottles joined the line of personal vehicles all heading out to the community. My cousin and I followed the trucks and joined them. Every square inch of my SUV filled. Trip after trip.

Strangers helped elderly, tired, dirty, sick, scared strangers pack all of their belongings into trash bags preparing to load buses for the Red Cross shelter at NRG Stadium. Their stories echoed through my high school halls. A chaotic cacophony of stories and worries, packing and moving, cleaning and loading filled the air.

Everything the whole family owned reduced to four trash bags.

My sister is coming, can I wait a few more minutes?

I think I found a hotel, please I'm not going to another shelter.

Why do we have to go? What will happen to us next?

The Red Cross is there at NRG Stadium.

They can get you the help you need.

Tony could barely walk. We packed his bags and carried them to the bus. He told us his story. My landlord's daughter, he said. I saw her front porch; it just floated away. They came for me in a boat, and here I am.

Lee was so worried about her dog and her things. She was walking in circles in shock. She was talking in circles in shock. I found her teenage son. Here, you may need this kennel when you get there, so the dog can stay with you.

She won't let Rosie go in there.

She may have to.

Will there be showers? Will they be private?

I don't know.

Do you have enough blankets?

A teenage girl begged, please can I keep this cat blanket?

You can have any blanket here you want.

Have you had lunch? Here's a slice of pizza.

Here's a chicken sandwich. Here's a bottle of water.

What do you need? How can I help you?

This mantra filled the walls of my alma mater coming from every age, race, creed, economic status.

This mantra filled my heart with hope.

Mom said the marines are in town.

I said praise God, all will be well, the marines have come.

The army came to Spring. Praise God, all will be well.

They loaded the remaining supplies after the evacuees left. Truckload after truckload piled into the back of their army vehicles and taken down to NRG Stadium. They stationed themselves in front of the Spring High School "Wall of Honor" for their briefing, and I choked back tears. Today, all law enforcement, first responders, military, and civilian helpers belong on the "Wall of Honor." Today, my hometown belongs on the "Wall of Honor."

As the storm raged, as a community waited for more permanent shelters to be established, Spring did not wait. In the blink of an eye, they served the least among us. Without hesitation.

Neighbor helping neighbor. Cor Unum. One Heart.

THE PUNISHER'S STORY

Well. Your cousins are on their way from San Antonio with this.

Dad held up his phone, and I laughed at the picture of a five-ton truck they purchased off Craig's List. The front of it was aptly painted "The Punisher."

I recalled an image that came across Facebook earlier of a man aiming his gun towards Hurricane Harvey, still off shore at the time. I thought to myself, which one of you is that? My brother, my cousins, which one of you is that out there? And I laughed at the thought of them all holding a line. I imagined my cousins bumping up and down on the highway getting that good old 2-50 AC Grandpa always joked about. You know. Two windows, fifty miles an hour. That was good air conditioning in Grandpa's truck. I imagined them joking about giving Harvey a beating as they headed into town on their Punisher. I imagined my brother, the Marine Corps veteran and police officer, now protecting his house and neighborhood. I imagined my cousin back in Iraq in battles unpredictable. In battles and images none of us could ever come close to fathoming. I imagined Grandpa back in the Pacific War in battles unpredictable. In battles none of us could ever come close to fathoming.

Watch out Harvey. Didn't you hear, the marines are in town.

And this marine came with his new truck, "the Punisher."

They drove in and out of the Addicks and Bear Creek area trip after trip bringing out people, pets, supplies. I saw them in a news story[6], and that family pride welled up. The boys I grew up with didn't wait, didn't think twice, didn't hesitate. As the storm raged and the waters rose, they did not wait. In the blink of an eye, they left their homes and families behind to rescue others. Without hesitation.

Stranger helping stranger. Cor Unum. One Heart.

THE CLEAN UP STORY

It wasn't until Harvey was well off into Louisiana or even Mississippi before I began to feel completely helpless. Began to feel that survivor's guilt, maybe. It was the first day I couldn't do anything but stay in my dry, clean house. All the frenzy of the past few days pushed me to the edge of bronchitis, and I had to stop. At least for a moment. There is too much to do for anyone to stay down. There is too much Houston Strong in all of us to stay down.

With sun shining and breeze blowing, those who could went out. They took power tools, wheelbarrows, shop vacs, cleaning supplies. They went to the homes of family, friends, and complete strangers to rip out the mildewing, rotting, reeking furniture, appliances, carpeting, and walls. It didn't matter who needed help, those who were able went. It seemed like there could not possibly be enough workers to go around. But God provides, God sustains, God lifts. God multiplies our offerings.

Those who couldn't work and clean prayed and cooked. We made lunches and snacks for bone-tired, soul-weary workers. We watched kids, so those stronger could help. They drove trucks filled with pallets of water bottles handing them to everyone they passed. A woman in Mom and Dad's neighborhood ran extension cords to the street and hooked up her washer and dryer. She ran a clothes line between her front yard trees. Then the all call went out in the neighborhood that the laundromat was open for anyone who lost their washer and dryer. Drop it off. She did their laundry while they hauled their ruined lives to the streets.

What was it like out there, I asked?

Every house on the street is filled with people ripping, tearing, clearing, cleaning. Piles upon piles of wreckage littered the yards and streets.

The Saint called midday. Defeated.

I'm headed to Home Depot, he said. I busted a pipe trying to rip out the cabinets. Water filled the house again. The main water-line shutoff busted in the flood. We rushed to the outside street cutoff. It is just trickling now. But there's water all through the house again. I'm getting a cap for the pipe. I'm getting a stronger wet-dry vac.

How is she doing, I asked?

Defeated. We are so tired. We just want to get done.

Often it has to get worse before it can get better. But two steps forward and one step back still keeps you moving. That is where we are today. Thursday. Is that today? Is it already Thursday? That is where we are today. Two steps forward and one step back in a dance to rebuild our city. Two steps forward and one step back in a dance to reclaim our city. Hope finally rising faster than the waters.

Neighbor helping neighbor. Houston Strong.

THE SCHOOL'S STORY

One of our school moms started a Facebook group for school network connections. Within a matter of hours there were over a thousand people joined from all over the country. Offers for coordinating donations, for keeping garages stocked with cleaning supplies to pick up, for help coming from out of town, offer after offer poured in. Home addresses posted as donation spots across the city. Drop whatever you can, pick up whatever you need, is all the post said. Donations in, supplies out, to all parts of the city. I stopped by to get supplies. A parent was dropping things off; another teacher, like me, was picking things up. Stuff for her sister's and mom's houses.

I don't want to be greedy, she said. There's just so much to do it's overwhelming. Her voice drifted reflectively into her own story. We had to evacuate, she said. The Coast Guard came and took us out in boats. Right before that we heard knocking, banging on the door.

Please, can we come in, came a voice from the other side. It came up so fast; we have nowhere to go. Please, can we come in? We let them in. What else would we do? They left their house and came running to our higher ground. Then the Coast Guard came, and we all left in a boat. What else were we supposed to do? They needed help.

I posted about needing a microwave, fridge, and help with cleanup for Baby Boy's family in Spring. Within five minutes I had more replies than I could process. More people than were needed to come help clean up. A microwave and two mini-fridges with the hope and promise of help to keep coming.

I'm getting the microwave, a teacher from school messaged me. Wait. And a griddle. Will she need this range top? Pictures came flying in before I could even respond. Yes, she said. She needs these; I'm getting them, and if not, someone will need it.

I posted I needed a mattress and box spring for a twin sized bed. Joy-Bearer called immediately. I'll find one. I'll put in a hundred dollars for it. Will that be enough to get you going? I'll call others. Do you have what you need?

All for a stranger. All for a woman who is not connected to this school family. A social awareness which impels to action does not discriminate against school family or not. A social awareness which impels to action reminds us that we are cor unum et anima una in Corde Jesus. We are one heart and one soul in the heart of Christ.

In this space of social media, we shared the light of Christ with each other and anyone we could help. We didn't wait, didn't think twice, didn't hesitate. As the storm raged, and the waters receded, and the stench rose, we did not wait. In the blink of an eye, we cleaned up our city. Without hesitation.

Neighbor helping neighbor. Cor Unum. One Heart.

BREATHING IN THE SIGHTS

I made is out again today. The smell hit you before anything else. Putrid. Rotting. Stench. The smell of lives turned upside-down filled the air ripping the breath from my lungs. The sight of lives turned upside-down filled the streets. Two lane roads were barely passable with one car. We drove in silence as if entering a war zone. Completely surrounded by parked cars. Some belonged to the countless helpers in the neighborhood. Many were destroyed by the flood, left as a constant reminder of the upheaval in Harvey's wake. My gut was in upheaval as I tried to keep my lunch inside. Walls of stuff filled the streets. Mildewing carpets. Appliances. Sinks. Drywall still saturated. Texas Strong Bluebell ice-cream cartons. Kids toys. They were the hardest to pass. Where are the children? There are no children to be seen here. Just broken, dirty toys littering the streets as a constant reminder of the littlest ones affected by Harvey's wake.

Where are all the children?

What little breath I had was stripped from me when I found her house. The same house I left them at Sunday night as I kayaked away was now gutted. A mountain of stuff littered her front yard. They came to tow her car. We couldn't even open the trunk. As they loaded it on the truck, water spilled out from the backside like the last bit of water that refuses to stay in after the hose has been turned off. There he was again. More of Harvey refusing to stop trickling. Reminding us everywhere of his fury.

The eyes were the worst. Shell-shock in every face you passed.

Empty. Hollow. Bone-tired, soul-weary, shell-shocked eyes.

I went to pick up a mini-fridge from my friend who just got back in town from Austin. She looked into my eyes. She shifted her feet and looked again. Deeper into my eyes this time.

What the hell are you looking for, I thought?

Then, I realized she couldn't find me.

I wore the same shell-shocked expression I had just come from. I was a tortoise retreating deep into my soul for respite, for safety, for comfort. We have become tortoises hiding in fear. We have become tortoises retreating to our places of safety. We have become our own islands.

She looked deep into my eyes and couldn't find me.

All she found were the empty, hollow, bone-tired, soul-weary, shell-shocked eyes of my neighbors.

Frog texted: I'm numb. I saw a picture of myself earlier today and didn't even recognize myself.

Send it, I said.

You have to promise to delete it if I do.

Promise kept. It's gone forever except in both of our memories. Sad, tired, empty eyes. Almost unrecognizable beyond the friend I can still find in there. Shining through. If I look deep enough. I sang *True Colors* over and over in my head as I prayed for her. Prayed for all of us as depression started to seep in. It's one of the five stages of loss, right? What will come next? Acceptance? Of what? Of a new normal? Of true colors?

Friend, I see your courage shining through. Yes, this season has made us crazy, given us all we can bear, but sad eyes, I know your smile is still in there. Don't be discouraged. It's our true colors, our courage, that makes us all beautiful like rainbows.

Sunshine texted: how is your asthma doing?

Alright now. I'm just tired, exhausted, weary like everyone else.

She said, you need to rest this weekend.

It won't happen friend. Cleanup. Taking a family in. Funeral. Back to work Tuesday.

She said, rest or this fall will be hell.

I said, it already is.

Despite the empty feelings of helplessness that start to engulf us, we push on. Driving around the city getting help from where we can. Bartering milk for medicine. Loading vehicles with supplies. Giving what we have to absolute strangers. Hauling filth upon filth to the streets. Preparing houses to be dried and rebuilt.

Without hesitation we are stranger helping stranger until stranger becomes friend. We are neighbor helping neighbor until neighbor becomes family.

Cor unum. One Heart.

We are Houston Strong.

We are Houston Tired.

SPRING
HIGH
SCHOOL
WALL OF HONOR

Clouds finally breaking (August 29, 2017)

~

Receding water lines (August 29, 2017)

Sunset (August 29, 2017)

Army trucks arriving (August 30, 2017)

Spring High School shelter donation piles (August 30, 2017)

Spring High School shelter cleanup (August 30, 2017)

Army water caravan (August 30, 2017)

Buses leaving for the Red Cross shelter NRG Stadium (August 30, 2017)

Loading Army trucks for the Red Cross shelter at NRG Stadium (August 30, 2017)

Donations for the Red Cross shelter at NRG Stadium (August 30, 2017)

Empty grocery shelves (images shared via family texts) Photo credit: unknown

~

"The Punisher" (images shared via family texts) Photo credit: unknown

"Pre-mucking" refrigerator toppled by the flood waters (images shared via family texts) Photo credit: unknown (August 31, 2017)

"Pre-mucking" floor boards ripped up by the flood waters (images shared via family texts) Photo credit: unknown (August 31, 2017)

House "mucking" day (images shared via family texts) Photo credit: unknown (August 31, 2017)

Cleared out kitchen (images shared via family texts) Photo credit: unknown (August 31, 2017)

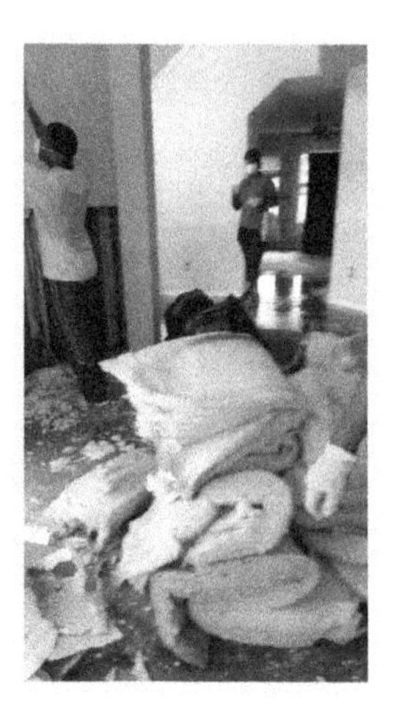

(images shared via family texts) Photo credit: unknown

House "mucking" trash pile (August 31, 2017)

Street debris (September 1, 2017)

"Garage Sale" of street debris (September 1, 2017)

~

Children's toys in street debris (September 1, 2017)

Cleaning supplies (September 1, 2017)

House "mucking" day (September 1, 2017)

More cleaning supplies (September 1, 2017)

Ready for de-humidifiers (September 1, 2017)

"Mucking" day lunch break (September 1, 2017)

"Neighbor helping neighbor" (September 1, 2017)

BlueBell Texas Strong (September 1, 2017)

Old Glory (September 1, 2017)

3

WAVES TOWARDS A NEW NORMAL

MOM SAYS THIS OUR NEW NORMAL.

I sit breathing my nebulizer treatment as I contemplate what that means. Nebulizer treatments make me feel defeated. They are the last-ditch effort to get my breathing above water.

Is that what our new normal is? Every achy bone, every tired soul working with every last breath to get back above water.

I think about the faces, my own included, that look at each other with empty shell-shocked eyes. About businesses that will leave our city. About residents that will leave our city. About people who will never get their lives back together. I think about the days, weeks, months ahead trying to find normal again. Is that what our new normal is? A constant state of fatigue and unknowns.

I think about neighbors helping neighbors. I think about a city that a week into hell still does not see color, creed, age, gender, class, disability. I think about a city that a week into hell only sees a brother. All we can see is a human person in need. In need of a boat, a roof over their head, just a beer and a chair. And I weep, finally. God, I plead, please let this be our new normal. A world where heaven has met hell, where love has triumphed over fear, where we have lived as one human family in one of the most diverse cities in the world. Please God, let this love of each human person be our new normal.

Only time will tell what the new normal is.

In the days, weeks, months ahead we will find just how Houston Strong we are. We will find out just how long we can remain Cor Unum. One Heart.

MOVING IN

When does someone stop being a stranger and become a friend? When does someone stop being a friend and just become family? Is it when you show up at their door in a kayak, and you don't even know their name? Or when they spend one night at your house, both of you shaken and traumatized in your own way? Maybe it is the night she joins your family for dinner at a Chinese buffet after a long day cleaning out her house, and you can all finally smile and laugh about the slowest FEMA representative known to mankind. Or, is it when she moves in for who knows how long? When does someone stop being a stranger and become a friend? When do they become family.

She rang the doorbell.

Well, she said. The homeless are here.

Not homeless friend. Welcome home. For as long as you need.

Please don't spend any FEMA money on a hotel. Please, stay here. You will need all that money and more just to put your house back together.

We made up a room for her with the new mattress and box spring. I moved the rocking chair in. That old worn rocking chair weathered three babies before becoming my favorite prayer chair. Its cushions molded to the shape of my body holding babies, rocking babies, praying over babies. She likes to pray, I said. She needs this prayer chair in her room. We made up a room for her sister and Baby Boy. I fought back tears as the Saint put that old crib back together. Oh, the stories that crib could tell. It was mine when I was a baby. Mom and Dad put it on layaway back in the days before credit cards and endless piles of debt. Harvey will rack up some serious debt. But not in this house. Not for our new family, if we can help it. A crib and some toys for Baby Boy. A cleared out top dresser drawer for diapers. A twin sized bed for his mom.

Not homeless friend. A home for as long as you need.

The Saint made dinner. We sat around the kitchen table in an awkward silence before the goofiness of children broke it. Middle-son said, why is it so quiet? An invitation for Younger-son to start talking not stop.

We laughed about the innocence of children and their unending energy. We laughed and talked. From two different worlds. Hers, black Mississippi. Mine, white Texas. Bonding over our common love of wine, teaching, and our Jesus. I think about neighbors helping neighbors. I think about a city that a week into hell still does not see color, creed, age, gender, class, disability. I think about a city that a week into hell only sees a sister.

Here on this temporary island, we find that out of the worst of nightmares hope and grace shine brightest.

TRYING TO MOVE ON

The cars smelled like armpits after hauling kayaks, wet people, and wet stuff for days. The whole garage smelled like armpits. We opened every car window and door to the sun and breeze. It is time to air out our armpits. Time to move on. The Saint and I go out every night at about eleven and take a deep breath of the cool September night air. Nope. Still here. The smell of rotting stuff fills the air. Maybe this is the new normal. Stench. And armpits.

There is an isolation these storms tend to create. Yes, we are so connected, so close to the strangers on our island. They have become new members of our family even. Welcomed in that moment where love triumphs over fear. Yet, we are so isolated from our most intimate friends just a city away. It is tempting to let the shell-shock eyes win out. But what good will that do anyone?

We have to go back to school soon.

The Saint said once the teachers go back, the kids have a safe place to be, and everyone else can start going back to work and get this city moving again.

I said I don't have it in me yet.

How can I just switch from this reality to that one in the matter of a commute to work? The world doesn't understand how much emotional energy teachers give their students. Your children become our children for eight hours every day.

I said I don't think I have it in me.

But once the teachers can go back, then our city can finally start moving again. A shout out to the unsung teacher heroes. Here's to all the teachers this week who are bone-tired, soul-weary and are the first line to get this city back moving.

Teachers, we are Houston Strong.

NEVER REALLY GONE

I close my eyes tightly. I want to see it again. I want to see that black wall moving closer to me. A whirling, swirling, thick black wall. Followed by a calm, tender voice, "Okay baby, let's go back inside." The voice of peace and protection in the eye of the storm. My first memory. The eyewall of Hurricane Alicia and Dad's voice. He held me on the roof of our small house as the eye of the storm passed right over us.

Our lives move with the rhythm of chaos and peace, storm and eye. Sometimes we see a storm coming. We anticipate it. Prepare for it. Other times, without warning, it blindsides us and knocks us to our knees. We cry out, "Lord, save us! We are drowning!" God, how can you sleep in this boat while we are being beaten and tossed from every angle? Lord, wake up! Help us! Save us! Make it stop![7]

Won't someone go wake up our Lord?

As the maelstrom encircles us, we hold tight to those moments, those memories, of calm respite as an eye passes over. We hold tight to our Lord who never leaves our boat. Be still. O ye of little faith. He rebukes the wind. He calms our storm. He rebukes our shaken faith. He calms our anxious fears. The voice of correction. The voice of peace. The voice of protection. In the calm of the storm. "O God, I believe, help my unbelief."[8]

And just when we think it is finished, we come to realize that storms leave a path of destruction and chaos in their wake. Exhausted and empty we must now take up the onerous task of cleaning up and finding order. We have to work through this period of imbalance, confusion, and restoration before we wake up one day and realize that by God's grace normalcy and balance have finally returned. The eye of the storm is no longer the rarity but the constant. And we can finally look back with trust and gratitude for the ways God held us through it all.

It is cyclical. Chaos and peace. Storm and eye.

Waves towards a new normal.

The emotions come in waves now too. Like the first warnings of a storm kissing the shore and sneaking back out. There are so many ups and downs that words fail to express them all. You find yourself vacillating. Fear. Anger. Confusion. Hopelessness. Fatigue. Pride. Amazement. Love. "But the greatest of these is love."[9] And we let each one wash over us. We soak it in and let it move right on. Like the waves kissing the shore and sneaking back out.

Mom says that's the thing about hurricanes; they never really ever leave you. The next storm brings waves of memories flooding back. In a matter of seconds, they are all back again. Ike. Rita. Allison. Alicia. Flooding back, mixing together into one blur of hurricane-hardy people. Of storm-weatherers. Of Texas Strong people, where neighbor helping neighbor flows thick in our veins. Where we become cor unum. One heart.

And we find that out of the worst of nightmares hope and grace shine brightest.

A hurricane fortune "storms make oats take deeper roots." (image shared via family texts) Photo credit: unknown

Airing out the smells (August 31, 2017)

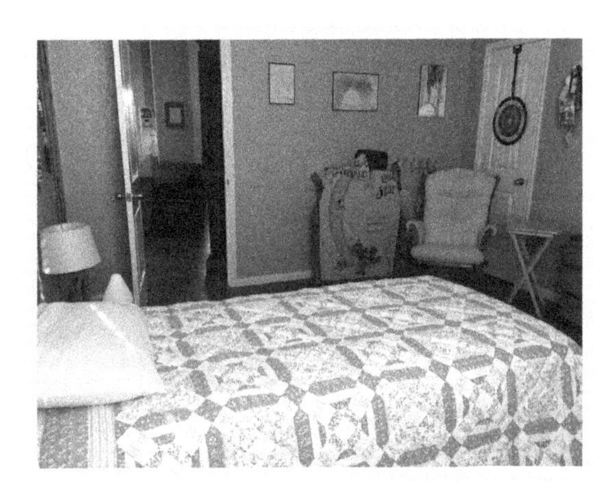

Moving in (September 2, 2017)

~

Room for two (September 2, 2017)

4

GOD, TIME, FRIENDS

IT'S THE FLAG. GETS ME EVERY TIME. DRAPED SO REGALLY. A testimony of a life of service and sacrifice. Precisely folded with gloved hands. They laid it in his daughter's lap. Tears streamed down my face as the memories flooded in. Taps. I'm a trumpeter. I could play it in my sleep still all these years later.

As Taps played, I was transported back to that frozen Tulsa ground. They laid the flag in Grandma's frail old hands. A testimony of a life of service and sacrifice. The gunshots pierced the frozen air. Cutting like knives through broken hearts.

No gunshots today. But in that bugle call, in that folded flag, the stifling, stale, after-hurricane Texas air met the icy Tulsa memories. I could hear the shots rip through the silence as my body shook back to this new normal.

We were bone-tired and soul-weary. Taps. Day is done. Gone the sun. From the lakes, from the hills, from the sky. All is well, safely rest, God is nigh. Yes. I believe all is well. God is nigh. We bowed our heads as the Preacher Man read from St. Paul. "Blessed be the God and Father of our Lord Jesus Christ, the father of compassion and God of all encouragement, who encourages us in every affliction, so that we may be able to encourage those who are in any affliction…for as Christ's sufferings overflow to us, so through Christ does our encouragement also overflow."[10] Amen.

Lord, we are a people who need encouragement. Today, in this new normal, we either need to be encouraged or need to encourage. We either need to be comforted or we need to comfort.

I searched Frog's shell-shocked eyes, and I found her. I found my friend in there. Hey, you with the sad eyes. Don't be discouraged. The God of all encouragement holds you close. He is the greatest comforter. I held her hand and didn't want to ever let go. Truth is I needed her healing comfort as much as she needed mine.

Preacher Man says three things will bring healing comfort:

God, time, and friends.

HEALING COMFORT

I about fell out of my seat when he eulogized his dad and referenced the 1960s movie "No Man Is An Island." Mom says we are all islands right now. But not anymore. As the waters recede, none of us are islands. Harvey shook us, but in this new normal we rediscover what we've known deep in our bones. No man is an island. We need each other. When prayer was all we could muster, all we could do, all we could hope with, we remembered that our God designed us to "rejoice in hope, endure in affliction, persevere in prayer."[11] When we felt like isolated islands, we took each other by the hand to "rejoice with those who rejoice and weep with those who weep."[12] Yes. All is well. God is nigh. No man is an island.

The emotions come in waves now. Like the first warnings of a storm kissing the shore and sneaking back out. There are so many ups and downs words fail to express them all. You find yourself vacillating.

I can't sleep at night. I keep hearing them calling for boats. I keep wondering what I am going to teach thirteen-year-olds when we go back to school, when I am so completely bone-tired, soul-weary myself. Then I think about all the walls we put up to protect ourselves and compartmentalize our lives. I think about the healing comfort of friends. No more neat walls. With each person we meet, with each story we tell, we enter into each other's messy lives.

"Christ has no body but yours, no hands, no feet on earth but yours. Yours are the eyes with which he looks compassion on this world, yours are the feet with which he walks to do good, yours are the hands with which he blesses the world."[13] And I think about the healing comfort of the body of Christ. In giving His comfort and humbling ourselves to receive His comfort. To and from each other. No more neat walls. Christ has no body now but yours.

I held her hand and didn't want to ever let go.

And I rejoiced in the healing comfort of God, time, and friends.

A DAY OF LABOR

"By the way, no one in Houston knows what day it is."

I laughed as that line flashed across my Facebook feed. And I thought, seriously, what day is it? The first Monday of September. Labor Day. Founded in the late 1800s to celebrate the rights of workers and the contributions laborers have made to our country. That national pride, that Houston Strong welled up inside as I thought about how different this Labor Day is. No pool parties. No backyard barbecues. Instead a day of labor to rebuild our city. A day of labor to reclaim our city.

The emotions come in waves now. Like the first warnings of a storm kissing the shore and sneaking back out. There are so many ups and downs words fail to express them all. You find yourself vacillating.

I took the rest of Mom and Dad's stuff home as the sun set on this Labor Day. As I turned the corner the smell of skunk filled my car. Is that skunk? No. It is landfill. All around me the sights and smells of landfill. My stomach churned.

Dad found me outside dry heaving.

You throwing up in my bushes Daughter?

No. Just heaving. It smells like death. Your neighborhood smells like death.

Welcome home Daughter. Welcome home where death fills the air. Can't stomach the smell?

No Dad. It's the emotions.

Yeah, he said, we all have them now.

Yeah, I said. My eyes have run dry. It's the emotions. Maybe I can vomit them out.

Come inside Daughter.

You need to drive around the neighborhood on your way out, Dad said as I got in my car to leave.

Why? I asked. I might vomit.

Because it's your neighborhood. It's your childhood. You need to see it all.

I might vomit.

You need to see it again, he said.

I turned the corner and saw him was sitting on his porch like always. The Marine under his flag.

I could have escaped this hell, but I listened to my churning gut and pulled over.

I just want to say…I kicked at the ground remembering Olderson teasing me just yesterday. Mom you can give amazing speeches to hundreds of people. He exaggerates. He's never actually heard me speak, and it certainly hasn't been to hundreds of people. Mom you can give amazing speeches to hundreds of people, but mom you can't even start a conversation with a stranger.

I kicked the ground.

Just wanted to say, I started again…I grew up over there on Artesia St…And well…I kayaked in to Mom and Dad's house for several days last week…And well…I just wanted to say your flag gave me hope each time I passed.

Steve, he said, the name's Steve.

Rachael, I said.

We shook hands. His old swollen calloused hands enveloped mine. We looked into each other's eyes telling our stories with no words.

You know why I fly it all the time?

No sir.

The national anthem by Francis Scott Key. You know that one?

Yes sir. My family is marines, too.

Semper Fi, he announced.

Semper Fi, I smiled.

By the dawn's early light. That's why it stays over my house all the time. While the battle rages on, by the dawn's early light, the first sight they saw was the flag. Still there. And here it is. Still here today.

Yes sir.

We looked into each other's eyes telling our stories with no words. And smiled.

Say. You going home to someone?

Yes sir. My husband and three boys and the family staying with us.

You don't look old enough to have kids, he said.

You're a charmer, I smiled.

I'm a marine, he laughed and winked. Take this food home then.

No sir. We have plenty.

The marines come each day and check on me. They help me clean up. They bring me food. They put all those flags out there in the yard. It's just me here. It's gonna go to my dog out back if you don't take it. Too much food for an old man by himself, he grinned.

We don't need it sir, thank you.

Well. Do you know someone who does? Say, why don't you drive around and find someone.

I might vomit, I thought.

Yes sir, I mustered.

Here take these mini flags to those at your house and don't be a stranger. And say, Rachael, give me a wave when you drive by will you?

Yes sir. Maybe I'll stop in and say hey sometime.

That'd be nice.

God bless you, sir.

God bless you, doll.

Semper Fi, I thought. I was Grandpa's doll.

Steve's story came rushing back to me blurring marine Steve and navy Steve and Grandpa into one mix of emotions. The emotions come in waves now. Like the first warnings of a storm kissing the shore and sneaking back out.

I drove around.

You have dinner, I asked?

Yes ma'am, they keep bringing us food.

House after house. Everyone fed. Filling me with Houston Strong pride. Until I saw them.

You have dinner?

Language barrier. Yeah, dinner he said in his broken English.

Oh, okay. Well, do you know someone who needs dinner?

Yeah. Yeah. Dinner. Four people.

Oh, you need dinner?

Yeah. Yeah. Dinner.

Here, this is from the marine around the corner.

She looked up from her work, tears welling in her eyes. Gracias was all she could muster.

De nada. Agua? Agua, you have agua?

Her son finally came out. Yes, we have water, he said clearly, we just need dinner.

God bless you then. I handed him the warm trays of sloppy joe sandwiches and mac n' cheese. And the bags of chips and brownies. Goodnight, and God bless you.

Tears streamed down her bone-tired, soul-weary, work-dirty face as I pulled away.

I fought back the tears as I drove out. I fought back the heaving as far as the baseball fields. I pulled over and heaved and vomited and heaved and vomited. Emotion after emotion flowing out with my rancid lunch into the park trash cans. Asthma. I hate asthma. Then I remembered it all. Baby Boy. Cancer. Steve. No, both Steves. Dinner-less workers on Labor Day. The Stench. Houston. Hurricanes. All of it. I sat beside my car and cried until there was nothing left to cry. Nothing left to vomit.

Dear God, please let this be the final purge. Let this be the last purge back to normal. Dear God, please. Only in You can we find normal. Restore us again, O God of our salvation.

Frog texted: how are you feeling?

I said I'm writing again. It's cathartic, I said. And I can't stop. I keep waiting for the happy ending. Friend, when will it turn happy? It is filled with so many ups and downs, mostly downs. I think I keep waiting for it to be uplifting. I can't stop.

It's coming, she said, it has too. Hang in there.

You too friend. All of us. Hang in there. It's coming.

Restore us again, O God of our salvation.

SLEEP

I still can't sleep at night. I don't know why. Things are okay. Things are moving on. Things are finding normal again. Aren't they? I try the essential oils in the diffuser like Frog said. Cedarwood and lavender. And I just lay here. Listening to the hum and trickle of the diffuser. I reached my arm out and put my hand on the Saint's shoulder. I just wanted to feel him. To touch him. To know he was there.

Therapist is going to want to talk about trauma.

I don't have trauma, I argued one time with her. Just formative events. We all have formative events.

But I want to talk about the present and the future, I tell her.

Because in the whole scheme of things, in the whole scheme of this hurricane, I don't have any trauma.

I've lost nothing.

Trauma doesn't equal loss, I know she's gonna say.

What is trauma?

Maybe we all have it right now.

Maybe we all have a little PTSD in us right now.

Those who've lost materials. They can be replaced. It's just things. It's just money. Until you have none.

Those who lost loved ones. Plagued by the guilt, the what ifs.

Those with survivor's guilt.

All of us are a little restless. Anxious. Sleepless.

Maybe we all have a little PTSD in us right now.

I still can't sleep at night.

Not sure I've consistently slept well since last February.

Since asthma took my breath so bad they put me in the hospital.

Sunshine texted: get some rest this weekend or this fall is going to be hell on your asthma.

It already is, I said. So, I reach out to touch the Saint just to feel him next to me. Just to know he's there.

Preacher Man says three things bring healing comfort:

God, time, and friends.

Preacher Man forgot sleep.

We all need a good, long, healing sleep.

Somewhere between dream and awake I heard it. Finally. We listened every night, and there it finally was. The train whistle cut through the early morning air. The low rumbling of wheels on the tracks. The trains have resumed their routes. Bringing us back, signaling a return to normal.

The cedarwood and lavender tease. Swirling and dancing around me. Eventually enveloping me like his old, swollen, calloused hands around mine as the *Moana* song plays again in my brain. Reminding me how far I can go. And I drift off with my mind's constant soundtrack rising a song of hope above this land of restless, sleepless nights.

Preacher Man forgot sleep.

God. Time. Friends. Sleep.

~

BACK TO SCHOOL

We found Older-son in the closet reading and crying at nine o'clock the night before we went back to school. In a panic. I didn't finish my reading log this week. I didn't finish it. It's a new school, and I'm going to get my first late assignment. You have to admire his diligence.

Baby. Stop please. Just listen. No teacher is taking work tomorrow. I promise. I just emailed one of my students the same thing. No teacher is taking work tomorrow. Baby. Stop please. Just listen. No teacher even remembers what she was teaching before all this. I promise. Tonight, every teacher just wants their students to go to bed early and have a good night's sleep. I promise.

He melted in my arms. Will you snuggle me, he pleaded?

I thought you'd never ask, I answered, as I climbed up to the top bunk. Older-son wrapped his arms around me. He's ten now, eleven next month. Almost the same size as me. We wear the same shoe size. He wrapped his arms tightly around me and wouldn't let go. I stroked his hair like when he was a child, and he finally drifted off to sleep.

No teacher is taking work tomorrow.

I held him tight and didn't want to ever let go.

She yelled at me, mom, because I didn't finish my reading log.

No, she didn't.

She did. But I told her why they weren't done, and she backed off.

He was chipper. He was happy dancing around the room. They were all chipper after the first day back. Chipper, happy, excited actually to have homework again. Going back to routine is a good thing.

Like the train rolling down the tracks, normal is coming back.

My day was not so chipper. I fought back tears at school. It was just us teachers. A chance as adults to regroup, talk, plan. I couldn't listen as they talked. I did not care one bit. I was numb. They talked about PTSD. How to recognize it in others. How to recognize it in ourselves. Maybe we all have a little PTSD in us right now.

A school can serve as a church, they said. As an institution of hope, they said. We are a church and sign of hope for the families when they return.

I tried to listen, but her voice echoed in my ears again over seven years later. I want you there, she said. You are the campus minister here, and this my church. You are my minister. He was her only son, her only child. Died. Suddenly. Violently. Texting and driving just weeks before his college graduation. I was a twenty-eight-year-old kid holding this mother's hand. She taught French in the room across the hall from me, and she desperately needed the comfort of God in another. We talked every day in my classroom. She called every night, and I hid in the closet to hear her over the din of a house of toddler boys. We talked and cried and prayed together.

I held her hand and didn't want to ever let go.

I want you there, her voice echoed in my ears. I want you to lead his graveside service. No one else from school, except her French department co-teacher. No one else. Just family and you. You are family, you know. You are my minister. We concluded with the Lord's prayer spoken together in the language of choice. His mother, aunt, and a few others in French. His best friend in Spanish. The rest of us in English. The mixing of language in a cadence of familiar comforting prayer. Cor unum. One Heart.

Two weeks later my family was in the worst car accident of my life. To avoid a major side swipe on the freeway, the Saint swerved, and our car went into a spin eventually hitting the concrete guard rail head-on at fifty miles per hour. The airbags deployed filling the car with toxic smoky powder. The Saint lost his glasses and shattered his phone. Adrenaline kicked in as I found his glasses, checked on crying kids, and crawled into the back of the car to find my phone. I collapsed into the front seat, handed him the phone, and said call me an ambulance. With head spinning and body aching, they strapped me to a backboard and took me to the hospital. By the grace of God, I walked out later that day just bruised, literally from head to toe. Head, lung, abdominal contusions some the size of two grown man's hands. Even a small bruise on my big toe. How does that even happen? Maybe his shattered phone found my foot, we laughed. Weekly checks for internal bleeding. Six months of physical therapy. But, by the grace of God I walked out just bruised, literally from head to toe.

And I thought of my friend. How is it that God allows one to live and another to die? How does a twenty-eight-year-old come to a place to bury a twenty-three-year-old and two weeks later walk away from the hospital?

A school can serve as a church, they said. As an institution of hope, they said.

I know that pain, I thought.

It is the stuff nightmares are made of.

Maybe we all have a little PTSD in us right now.

We went to lunch after the meetings. Just us teachers.

Joy-Bearer made us all a comfort food dessert to lift our spirits.

I texted Sunshine: save me a seat, I want to sit by you.

I wanted the comfort of her presence. I wanted my friend.

One teacher looked at me and said, I wanted to ask if you come here a lot, if I could buy you a drink.

I laughed. I must look bad.

I felt my face melting to a new normal.

Not so distant. Not so shell-shocked.

Maybe we're gonna be okay. All of us here in this moment.

Sunshine grabbed my hand earlier that morning in chapel.

I held her hand and didn't want to ever let go.

Preacher Man says three things bring healing comfort:

God, time, and friends.

HOW ASTHMA ACTUALLY HELPED, FOR ONCE

I felt anxiety rising and choking my breaths. No. Not now, I pleaded. I had this appointment for weeks. Well before Harvey was even a blip on the radar. Well before I felt it coming. Deep in my chest. An ache. A growing tightness, like a human barometer. Well before I spent the past two weeks fighting asthma with every breath and strength in my body. It was my last appointment with her. She who helped me understand this chronic hell called asthma. She who walked me through the ups and downs of inhaler after inhaler until we found the right one for me. She who counted the minutes deciding if I was to go by ambulance or if the Saint would make it in time to take me to the hospital. She who called me just to check and see how things were going. She who fought tears when I came for my post-hospital follow-up. It was my last appointment with her before she stepped out of practice for a while to focus on being a mom. And I wanted with every breath in me to be strong. To be well. I felt it coming. Deep in my chest. An ache. A growing tightness. I fought the good fight for two weeks now, and I am bone-tired, soul-weary, asthma-exhausted.

Look me in the eyes, she said. You can't save the world.

I melted.

You have to take care of yourself. Look me in the eyes. You have severe asthma. You can't be stubborn. You can't ignore it. You will end up back in the hospital, and I can't be there with you this time. You have severe asthma, and it is complicated and messy and takes you down fast.

Like a hurricane, I thought. Complicated, messy, destructive, fast.

You have to get well, she said. You have fought hard for two weeks, and you are winning, for now. But the air is bad. And the mold. And the stress. And it will take you down hard and fast if you are not careful, and I cannot be with you this time. And they need you to be well. All of them. Your husband. Your boys. Your students. Your friends. I need you to be well, she said. You can't go into any more house rebuilds. The mold and dust are terrible for you. You can't go into any more shelters. You will get a virus and end up really sick. I need you to be well, she said.

In that space she gave me permission to grieve. To grieve hurricane destruction and chaos. To grieve asthma. To grieve the loss of an amazing doctor-patient relationship.

I had a short list, she confessed.

I'm not supposed to, but well...you know.

Yes. Teachers don't have favorite students either, I winked.

Her eyes brightened and laughed.

Yes. She said. So, you know. I have a short list, and I'm not supposed to say this, but you were on the top. I looked for your name, and if you hadn't come to me, I would have called you.

I know. I wouldn't have not come.

You will be okay, she said. It feels like so much around us right now is out of control. You will be okay with all of it, if you take care of yourself first. Make sure you are filled before you try to pour anymore. There's a doctor I recruited to the practice a few years ago; she'll be good for you, she said. She's a bit of a drive, but she's worth it.

I know a doctor who will always be worth my drive, I said.

She smiled. I will only be out of practice for a little while, she said. Just until I get this mommy stuff balanced. I can't call you when I come back, it's not professional. Look me up in a year or so, will you?

I will, I said. I will.

We hugged each other tight and fought back the tears.

I hugged her tight and didn't want to ever let go.

When you go home tonight, she said. Let your husband take care of the boys. I want you to take a long, hot bath and go to bed early. Doctor's orders, she said. She is brilliant, in a simple, practical, loving way. And I'm going to miss her terribly.

I watched the water rising as I filled the tub. I thought about how that tub was last filled in preparation for the hurricane. I thought about the wind, rain, floods. I climbed in and watched the waters rise around me. Relaxing every tight muscle. Wrapping my whole body in warmth and comfort. Water is powerful; it is a destructive death-dealing force of nature. Water is powerful; it is God's gift of cleansing, healing, and life.

"In the beginning, when God created the heavens and the earth, the earth was without form or shape, with darkness over the abyss, and a mighty wind swept over the waters."[14]

Out of the darkness, God brought the light.

Water is life. Water is birth.

Water is new life and new birth in God.

I sank deep into the tub and let the water wash over me. It is time to let this hell called Harvey die. It is time to be cleansed of this destruction, suffering, pain, loss, stench. It is time to be cleansed of these shell-shocked, sad eyes. It is time to finally, really, let hope rise higher than the waters.

I sank deep into the tub and let the water wash over me. It is time to rise out of the waters and back into God's grace. It is time to rise out of the waters, not to a new normal, just back to normal. Because normal is blessed. Normal is grace. Water is cleansing. Water is purifying. Water is healing comfort.

Preacher Man says three things bring healing comfort:

God, time, and friends.

Preacher Man never met my asthma doctor.

ROUTINES AND SCHEDULES

Beep. Beep. Beep. My alarm sounded at five a.m. I wanted to throw my phone against the wall. As I drug myself out of bed, my body ached with fatigue. Can we really be going back to school today?

Teacher, how are you? How is your house? Can I just have a hug? Thirteen-year-old girls really are the most interestingly amazing creatures on the planet. Often stuck in their own world and drama, they never cease to amaze me with their wit, humor, smiles, love, and resilience. They are good medicine.

The bell summoned us to prayer, to class, to lunch. The bell summoned us all day long back to normal. Like the train rolling down the tracks, normal is coming back.

Teacher, it's September now, they reminded. We need a new precept for the month. Thirteen-year-old girls. One thing you can count on is that they are creatures of habit. They crave routines, structures, a sense of what is to come, what to expect. They are good medicine. The precept for September: "Joy is what happens when we allow ourselves to see how good things really are."[15] I write it on the board. A mantra more for myself than my resilient students.

I texted Frog that night: you doing okay friend?

I'm doing ok, she answered. Slowly starting to feel like myself again. I was driving home and caught myself singing to the radio. Made me realize how I hadn't sung in a long time, and I burst into tears. Because for one, brief moment I forgot everything and was just driving along and singing. And I had dreams for the first-time last night. Well, more nightmares, I guess. But, I realized if you don't sleep, you don't dream. How are you?

I don't know. It comes in waves you know. I was finally hungry today at lunch. Ravenous, actually, because I haven't eaten dinner in days. I was smiling with the kids and joking. But I haven't sung yet, come to think of it. And I still get lost in the flashbacks and have to bring myself back. But I can bring myself back. That is progress. So, I guess two steps forward and one step back is okay for now. Two steps forward, even with one step back, still keeps you moving.

It feels good that sense of routine. To know what to expect. To get back on a regular sleep and meal schedule. We are all creatures of habit. Sunrises. Sunsets. Alarms. Bells. Trains. Songs on the radio. As the days and weeks push by, we come to realize that routines and schedules offer healing comfort.

Are you taking notes yet? I'm taking notes.

God, time, friends, baths, sleep, routine.

Healing comfort.

Beltway flooding humor: "No Lifeguard on Duty" (image shared via FaceBook posts) Picture credit: unknown (September 4, 2017)

Beltway sign down but still flooded the next day on my way to the asthma doctor (September 5, 2017)

Street debris (September 4, 2017)

Street debris (September 4, 2017)

Street debris at Marine Corps Steve's house (September 4, 2017)

Semper Fi (September 4, 2017)

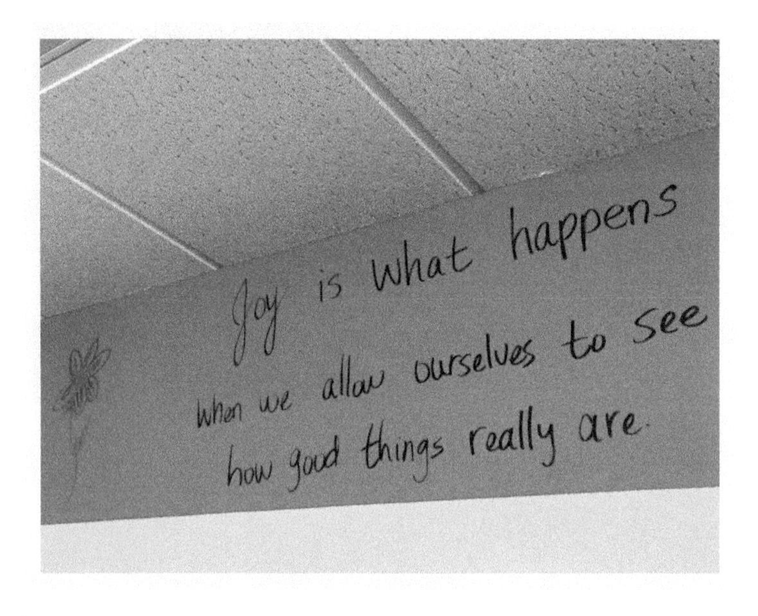

September precept (September 6, 2017)

5

BREATHING AGAIN

I WAS LYING ON THE COUCH RESTING WHEN THEY WALKED IN. I startled them. They didn't expect me there.

Well, we're moving out, she declared. Getting out of your way.

You have not been in anyone's way. Please stay, stay as long as you need. I wasn't ready for them to go. Not quite yet. Are you sure the housc is ready to be back in, I asked?

Well your dad and uncle got the doors on today and the sheet rock is out. It's dry in there. No mold. And we have the upstairs all cleaned up and fine. Just no hot water, yet.

What about dinner, I asked? Come back for dinner. Come back for dinner and a hot shower at least and to say goodbye to the boys. It's pizza Thursday, I said. You can't pass up pizza Thursday.

Pizza Thursday, huh, she said. We'll take our stuff back home and come by for dinner and a hot shower. See you soon.

See you soon.

Pizza Thursday. We haven't had pizza Thursday since the night before this thing came barreling in. We haven't had pizza Thursday in two weeks. Thursday. Thursday is dance night. No more dance for a while; the YMCA went under water. Thursday is dance night. No more dance for a while; asthma is rearing its ugly head. But pizza Thursday is back heralding another return to normal.

They came back for pizza dinner and hot showers. The kids ran around goofing off. Playing one more night with Baby Boy. We passed around shots of tequila. Mom says you learn a lot about a person over drinks. I don't know much about our stranger family after this whirlwind. But I do know that they are good, hard-working, honest people just trying to get by.

Well. I don't know if I can ever thank you for your hospitality.

Please don't. We are glad you came here.

When it's all done, we'll have to get some drinks, she said.

Mom says you learn a lot about a person over drinks.

I would like that, I said. I would like that a lot.

I hugged her as she left.

I hugged her tight and didn't want to ever let go.

The house was quiet. Eerily quiet after they left.

Silence filled my usually chaotic halls.

Is this the new normal, I thought? Then I heard it.

Mooooooooommmmmmm!!!

How do they do that?

How do they stretch my name into five syllables?

Mooooooooommmmmmm!!! He hit me!!!

Ahhh. Yes. There it is.

The sound of normal.

Normal finally rising faster than any flood waters.

A TEXAS STORY

The whole thing seemed so surreal, like a dream we all waited to wake up from. We are a hurricane-hardy city, but never have we seen the likes of Harvey. As the news droned on day after day, I began to wonder when will we wake up. Until I realized, we were awake. And this was our new normal. Our moment to show the world what it means to be Houston Strong.

Sun shining, water receding, Old Glory flying. No color, no creed, no difference. Just one human family. Brought together by devastation. Immeasurable devastation. Unthinkable losses. Unspeakable losses. Losses buried so deep in our hearts we cannot share them. Despite all this, we remain stranger helping stranger. Neighbor helping neighbor. Driven by the sense that we are all connected as one human family here to help each other. Driven by the assurance that hope always rises above the waters. Cor Unum. One Heart. And I hope we never wake up from this dream of Cor Unum. Achieved for a split second in time when the whole world stood still and loved each other as He loves us.

In spite of hurricane Harvey, we take hands, dry off our boots, and reclaim our city. In the end, we find that through the most disheartening of times hope and grace and the resilience of Texans shines brightest. They say everything is bigger in Texas. The Punisher certainly is. But this truth rings clear as we find that our new normal is what we've known all along. As we pull our boots up each day, we find there is a strength so deeply rooted in the spirit of Texans that we face our storms waving our flag: "Come and Take It!" Smirking behind our bone-tired, soul-weary eyes, knowing, come hell or high water, your neighbor's got your back. Come hell or high water, we have been and always will be Texas Strong.

WORKING IT OUT

Sunshine turned the lights off and sat on the floor in my classroom with me when the buildup finally came to a head. When the ups and downs of the past few weeks hit out of nowhere.

Come on let's get lunch, she said.

Wait. Crap. What's up? You're not coming to lunch, are you?

No. Can't breathe again friend.

She called the Saint. You need a doctor, she said.

No, I protested. I don't have one anymore. She's gone.

Sunshine sat next to me. Her hand on my knee, my tear-filled face resting against her shoulder. I know, she said patting my knee. I know you are afraid, she said. Close your eyes and try to breathe. You will be okay. I promise.

Another round of prednisone. The ultimate defeat with asthma. Another round of prednisone. That horrible, miracle-working drug. The fourth round in eleven months. Can't keep going like this, the doctors say. Need a more aggressive treatment plan, they say. The hurricane melted away as I let that reality start to sink in. Just one more thing to push me down.

Frog texted me reflections about God's immense love for me. About God loving me more than I can ever fully understand. Frog texted me reflections about trusting in His plan for my life. About trusting that He will show me how to make the right choice when faced with difficult decisions. I texted Frog: I don't know how you did it, but maybe you finally found a way to love me with asthma when I still can't love me with asthma.

The Saint patiently loved me as the steroids healed my lungs but tortured my body, mind, and soul. He bore the roller coaster of fears, agitations, annoyances, and my need to pick arguments. He walked with me when I felt unlovable, weepy, ugly.

They walked with me when I didn't like myself.

And this time, I finally let them.

I haven't felt like me in weeks.

Still trying to navigate the chaos of storms physical and emotional, literal and figurative.

Frog texted that she might be going to work out.

I did not want to go. Period. Did. Not. Want. To. Go.

I texted Frog: I'll work out if you do. Text me if you don't go.

I secretly prayed she wouldn't go. I hadn't worked out in six weeks. Not since the YMCA went under water and we had to find classes at different YMCAs all around the city. Not since asthma started rearing it ugly head again.

I did not want to go.

Frog texted back: guess who is teaching?

Yep. Guess who finally went to a workout again?

I started setting up the weights, and everything felt lighter. Body-pump on steroids I laughed to myself as I set up the next weights higher. Everything felt lighter. Pretty sure I'll regret this later, I thought.

Frog is a great teacher. Maybe I'm biased, but she really is the best. She, whose heart was still breaking, reminded us rep after rep that we may get pushed down, but we don't stay there, we rise up. Yes, everything, physical and emotional, literal and figurative, everything felt lighter. She chose her favorite mix. Maybe I'm biased, but it is always encouraging. We worked out to songs reminding us not to worry, songs about breaking free, songs about heaven's plan for us. And everything felt lighter.

As we walked out of the gym, Frog sighed.

I finally for a minute there felt like myself. I felt like me, she said.

Me too, friend.

I hugged her tight and didn't want to ever let go.

And so, we worked it out one day, one prayer, one rep, one step at a time. Pushing up, pushing out, rising up to that place where everything feels lighter.

RESILIENCE

I looked it up in the dictionary; I'm tired of the up and down cloud. I rose of the waters of Harvey. I rose up from the fog of an asthma flare. It is time.

Resilience: "the capacity to recover quickly from difficulties. Toughness."[16] Therapist says you're not weak; you're vulnerable. There's a difference.

I wonder can I be tough and vulnerable at the same time?

Is that possible?

Is that resilience?

Those few short weeks saw continued suffering. Continued fear. Harvey. Deaths. Asthma. More hurricanes. Fires. Floods. Earthquakes in Mexico. Threats of war. Mass shootings. Individuals suffering. Families suffering. A world suffering. And we find that we are not just Texas Strong, we find the strength and resilience of the human spirit rises faster than any flood waters. The resilience of the human spirit shines brighter than any darkness.

And we find that out of the worst of nightmares hope and grace shine brightest.

Out of the worst of nightmares the resilience of the human spirit overcomes.

But where does it come from?

Is it innate? Are some born more resilient than others?

No.

It is born in faith, when we can finally say, "Lord, I believe, help my unbelief."[17] When in both the storm and the eye, we say with confidence: Jesus, I trust in you.

It is born in hope, when out of fear we rise to new places of peace and assurance. When through the darkest tunnels, we can walk with confidence knowing the light will be there.

It is born in love, when we allow ourselves to recognize we are connected, we need each other, we encounter Christ in each other. It is born in the love of neighbor helping neighbor. Cor unum et anima una in Corde Jesus. One heart and one mind in the heart of Jesus.

"And the greatest of these is love."[18]

Resilience is born out of the ashes of suffering. Without suffering there is no growth. No joy. No redemption. Resilience is born when we can look to our God and praise Him knowing "tears may last for the night, but His joy comes in the morning."[19]

ALL WILL BE WELL

I remember clearly the day I could breathe again. Really breathe again. A deep, cleansing, invigorating breath.

I remember clearly the day the fog and haze lifted, and I could think again. Really think. Organized, coherent thoughts that formed a sense of structured meaning out of the chaos.

I remember clearly the day I could pray again. Really pray. Not just words, but a peaceful quiet with that still small voice reminding me to whom I belong and that "He will work all things for good for those who love Him."[20]

It was the day I read her reflection in my prayer book. It was the day a 14th century English mystic reached across the confines of time and spoke to a hurting 21st century world.

I walked into school and told the Boss Man I was going to need the microphone at morning prayer. I had something to say. Rather, my friend Julian of Norwich had something to say. How her words, centuries later, can still ring true for the young and old alike can be explained by the grace of God alone.

So, I took the microphone and declared to the young and old, the victim and survivor, the bone-tired and soul-weary, her vision:

> "God said to me: you won't be overcome. And these words were said so adamantly, and I was convinced. They gave me certainty and strength against every tribulation that might come.
>
> God didn't say you won't be attacked or you won't be overwhelmed or you won't be upset or you won't be stressed out. No, instead, He said, you won't be overcome.
>
> God wants us to pay attention to His words, and always be strong in our certainty—when things are going well and when things are going terribly—God wants us to love Him and delight in Him and trust Him with all our heart, and all will be well."[21]

And all will be well.

God, time, friends, baths, sleep, routine.

Healing comfort.

Resilience.

That place where breath meets flood.

Breath of God

Flood me with your presence

And all will be well.

Continued nebulizer treatments (September 7, 2017)

~

On the couch with Baby Boy's dog "Pepper Jack" the night they moved back home (September 7, 2017)

Still cleaning up the streets (September 16, 2017)

Still cleaning up the streets (September 16, 2017)

He Is Risen !

EPILOGUE

FOUR MONTHS LATER

~

GRATITUDE

Four months later and that house on the corner of Mom and Dad's street still has not been mucked out.

The owners are a young married couple from New York in a finance-by-owner situation. Moved down here to Spring to start up their restaurant business. We ate once at the Italian place in Old Town Spring, but we haven't made it to the Mediterranean place. The Italian was good, quaint, family friendly, but I hear it didn't make it. The restaurant business is a tough market. I wish now we had gone back more. Neighbor helping neighbor, you know. But, raising a family today is a tough market, too. The couple researched the area and came to our part of the city to make their new start as a young family.

Mom stood on the street with them that Sunday afternoon as the water rose and my sister and I blew up her phone pleading for them to leave. We later found out she ignored us because already Mom was neighbor helping neighbor. She started by reassuring them that in forty-five years the house has never flooded. Reassurances faded as they began taking steps back every five minutes. The water rose that fast on Sunday afternoon. Forcing the conversation further and further up the street. Forcing the young couple to grab a few things and head to another neighbor's house. Forcing Mom and Dad to call us to bring the kayaks. In all the chaos, Mom lost contact with them. By the next morning the house on the corner of the street where I grew up had water up to the roof.

Debates rage as to whose responsibility that property is. The owners financing it out or the young couple who signed a finance by owner contract? Regardless, four months later and that house on the corner of Mom and Dad's street still has not been mucked out.

The grass is overgrown. The brick mailbox leans at a forty-five degree angle threatening to collapse in a heap of rubble any day. Mold and moss grow up the outside of a once white house. Mold, no doubt, has overtaken the whole house.

Four months later that dark, empty, silent house stands as a reminder of dreamers and fighters, of painful endings and new beginnings, of the constancy of change. It stands as a reminder to be grateful for your blessings and pray for those, four months later, still just trying to figure it all out.

Four months later and the main buildings at the YMCA stand virtually untouched. Dark, empty, silent. Like these winter nights, they lie in deep slumber awaiting the springtime.

But beyond these silent gutted buildings lies one small, temporary, repurposed building. Four months later and my YMCA family has a humble space to workout the residual sufferings, losses, fears, and pains of the past few months. We don't have to travel all over the city in search of an open facility anymore. Here, we share our stories, and in our after-workout glow, we leave smiling. We leave filled. We leave with new strength for the coming springtime.

Four months later and we went to Sunday mass at St. Ignatius.

Like the YMCA, you have to drive past their dark, empty, silent buildings to get to the big white tent that stands as their temporary church home.

I remember the images of their flooded sanctuary when the video of their pastor, knee deep in flood waters, spread like wild fire around social media. Sacred space under water. Statues broken. A community scattered. I remember searching their pastor's eyes. I replayed that video over and over searching him deeper and deeper only to find the same shell-shocked, empty eyes we all wore in those days.

All the parishes on the north side watched their church.

Our hearts broke and cried for them.

Cor unum. One heart.

"And Jesus wept."[22]

"But they were not to be like sheep without a shepherd."[23]

Four months later and their pastor has a gift made out of remnants of his storm flooded church to deliver to the Holy Father. A sign of hope for his flock and all of us who look on. With each social media update, their pastor inspires courage in us all. We went to mass there today, and in spite of the silent sanctuary next door, the white tent beckons worshippers with a new revival. Songs of praise reverberate off these temporary walls. Parishioners share their stories. They are fed at His table. They leave smiling. They leave filled. They leave with new strength for the promised springtime.

In both places you find a new spark, a new twinkle, the beginnings of smiles. The real smiles are coming back, the ones marked by a spirit of hope and joy. Here in these broken places, these temporary spaces, hope triumphs.

Here, four month later, gratitude consumes us. Gratitude, the first fruits of suffering, hope, and resiliency, is palpable.

COMFORT

They went back to her house this weekend to help haul extra sheet rock away to someone else. Yep. A lot of people still just waiting for some sheet rock.

I have a student that after starting to rebuild found mold in the house again. She's allergic. They had to move out. Again. Four months later back on couches living out of suitcases. Lots of people still living without walls. The structure and safety of walls is comforting, and they don't even have that physical or emotional reassurance yet.

She does. And floors and some furniture, and they worked to hook up the gas line for her new stove. Four months later and she can finally start cooking in her kitchen again.

She's lucky. My brother can't yet. He's got floors and walls but no kitchen. They still eat out every night. They came to Spring to visit a few weeks ago, and I have never seen anyone so grateful for home cooking. We think eating out is a luxury; four months later and all they want is a home cooked meal.

So, I count my blessings.

I think each night about what I am grateful for that day.

Gratitude, they say, is the root of joy.

So, I try to be grateful for a smell, a mundane chore, a smile, a meal. For the strength that comes in rising up and the comfort of my God, my home, my people.

Four months later and a storm raged tonight. Wind. Hail. Rain. The whole nine-yards. I hadn't thought much of storms in a while. It was one of those winter cold fronts that push through. And my lungs held out. Those crazy, asthma-riddled, unpredictable things usually flare up and make me terribly uncomfortable with storms and changing weather. They hate change just like the rest of us. But they're holding strong. For now.

I count my blessings.

The Code-man barked at every lightning strike and every thunderclap echoing through the once still night. I tried to remember, did he bark like this in August? I can't remember him barking through that endless storm. He does not like this storm one bit. He climbed up in the bed and curled his sixty-five-pound body up at my feet finding comfort, solace, peace in his people.

I'll never forget when we got that dog.

It was three years ago this time of year.

Right around the new year.

Mom called: you have three kids and a ten-year-old dog. We picked up a stray dog. We can't keep him. He needs to be yours. Come get him, or we have to take him to the shelter. They picked him up running down a busy street and had already spent several days trying to track down an owner. Others knew about him. He had been missing for about three weeks. In and out of different neighbors' care.

Oh, the guilt. We had a ten-year-old rescue: Jackson. We were a one dog family. Didn't need two. But, I went over to Mom and Dad's house, and that dog captured my heart.

He was sorely underweight, but you could see a spark in his eyes and a raw beauty in his build. He was well-mannered and trained, even with Younger-son who wasn't even three at the time. So, I took him home to see how our territorial mutt would take to him. We started calling him New Dog and Big Baby, because we just couldn't commit. The day he responded to New Dog, I knew. He had found his home. He needed a proper name. Back and forth we went. Perhaps a theme with Jackson, the old mutt?

Cody, Older-son confidently declared.

Like Wyoming? I said, trying to find a connection to Jackson.

No mom.

Eye roll.

Commander Cody from Star Wars.

Who??

Oh yes, the loyal clone commander to Obi Wan in the Clone Wars who tragically succumbed to his dark programming in the end. A loyal sidekick with a troubled past. Seems fitting, so long as there is no Order 66 to execute. And so, three years and twenty more pounds later, the Code-man is a magnificently beautiful animal. He won't go outside without Jackson, prefers to eat when I sit at the breakfast table, and looks for anyone to snuggle up with starting at eight o'clock every night.

A loyal, faithful companion indeed.

And we begin to wonder who rescued who here.

Who comforts who here.

His is a story of overcoming and rising up just like the rest of us.

And he exudes gratitude in his chance to breathe again.

I texted Frog: There was a time when it rained like this that I used to hope maybe it would flood some streets, just some streets, and they would cancel school for the next day. A little surprise gift in the middle of the year. But not anymore. At least not for a while. I don't like this kind of rain still. Not one bit. And I used to like it. I used to find it comforting. I used to like to fall asleep to it. Not anymore. At least not yet.

Four months later and she doesn't really want to talk about it.

I'm not sure any of us really do.

It is now just a silent bond of hope that unites us.

A silent scar of knowing.

I told the Saint the same thing.

Nope, he said. Storms aren't quite the same yet, are they?

It was late, but there I was just like my Code-man finding comfort, solace, peace in my people. Some things I guess remain: God, time, and friends. Faith, hope, and love, and the greatest of these is still love.[24] And the comfort of my Saint next to me, my kids sleeping in the next room, and my Code-man curled up warming my feet as a cold front pushes through.

Four months later and we keep rising up.

We keep breathing.

Again.

"We even boast of our sufferings,
knowing that suffering produces endurance,
and endurance, proven character,
and proven character, hope,
and hope does not disappoint,
because the love of God has been poured out into our hearts
through the Holy Spirit that has been given to us."
--Romans 5:3-5

Winter snuggles with Cody (January 2018)

A winter storm (January 2018)

A faint double rainbow in a winter storm (January 2018)

Winter snuggles with Jackson (January 2018)

Unmucked house on the corner (June 2018)

A gift from Joy-Bearer (June 2018)

A neighborhood sunset (June 2018)

WORKS CITED

1. Christina Rasmussen, *Second Firsts: Live, Laugh, and Love Again* (New York, Hay House Publishing, 2013).
2. John 11:35
3. Matthew 8:23-26
4. Matthew 25:34-40
5. John 6:5-13
6. Elizabeth Flock, "For three brothers Texas pride means buying a 5-ton truck on Craigslist & helping fellow Texans," *PBS Newshour*, August 31, 2017.
7. Matthew 8:23-26
8. Mark 9:24
9. 1 Corinthians 13:13
10. 2 Corinthians 1:3-5
11. Romans 12:12
12. Romans 12:15
13. Attributed to St. Theresa of Avila
14. Genesis 1:1
15. Maryanne Williamson, *A Woman's Worth* (Random House Publishing Group, 2013).
16. Google dictionary
17. Mark 9:24
18. 1 Corinthians 13:13
19. Psalm 30:5
20. Romans 8:28
21. Julian of Norwich, "Strong in Certainty," *Give Us This Day*, September 2017, 197-198.
22. John 11:35
23. Matthew 9:36
24. I Corinthians 13:13

ABOUT THE AUTHOR

Rachael Valka has a bachelor's degree in theology and a master's degree in education from the University of St. Thomas, Houston. She is the campus minister and teaches theology at Incarnate Word Academy, an all girls high school in Houston. Before joining the IWA community, Rachael taught at Duchesne Academy and in July 2017, just six weeks before Hurricane Harvey hit, spoke at an international Spirituality Forum for the Society of the Sacred Heart. Much of this book is infused with Sacred Heart spirituality.

Rachael married her husband, the Saint, in 2004. They have three boys and two dogs. When not teaching girls by day and chasing her energetic sons by night and weekends, she enjoys respite in reading, writing, working out, praying, time outdoors, and moments of God's grace over coffee with friends.

"Breathing Again" is Rachael's first book. However, she hopes to one day publish her collection of poetry and prose. These "Red Light Writings" connecting everyday life moments with faith and universal human themes often come in quiet moments of the day like at stoplights or in the middle of the night when most of our brains can't seem to be still.

For updates or to contact Rachael:
Facebook: Red Light Writings
Email: RedLightWritings@gmail.com

CPSIA information can be obtained
at www.ICGtesting.com
Printed in the USA
LVHW011716161118
596837LV00011B/288

9 780692 162538